Alfred's max

Ukulele

MW00562615

see it • hear it • play it

RON MANUS
L. C. HARNSBERGER

Alfred's MAX™ is the next best thing to having your own private teacher. No confusion, no frustration, no guesswork—just lessons that are well paced and easy to follow. You listen to the music you're learning to play and watch a professional show how it's done, then get time to stretch out and put it all together. No matter how you like to learn, Alfred's MAX™ series gives you the ultimate learning experience at a screamin' deal of a price.

Ukuleles courtesy of Jennifer Harnsberger, jhphotostudio.com.

Alfred Music Publishing Co., Inc.
P.O. Box 10003
Van Nuys, CA 91410-0003
alfred.com

Contents printed on 100% recycled paper.

ISBN-10: 0-7390-8702-9 (Book & DVD)
ISBN-13: 978-0-7390-8702-2 (Book & DVD)

2

CONTENTS

About the DVD

The DVD contains valuable demonstrations of all the instructional material in the book. You will get the best results by following along with your book as you watch these video segments. Musical examples that are not performed with video are included as audio tracks on the DVD for listening and playing along.

The track numbers in the book refer to the MP3 audio tracks found on the DVD-ROM. These tracks are accessed by placing the disc in your computer. Windows users, from your Start menu, open My Computer, right-click on your DVD drive icon, and open the MP3 folder. Mac users, double click on the DVD icon on your desktop, then double-click on the MP3 folder.

SELECTING YOUR UKULELE

Ukuleles come in different types and sizes. There are four basic sizes: soprano, concert, tenor, and baritone. The smallest is the soprano, and they get gradually larger, with the baritone being the largest.

Soprano   **Concert**   **Tenor**   **Baritone**

Soprano, concert, and tenor ukuleles are all tuned to the same notes, but the baritone is tuned differently. Each ukulele has a different sound. The soprano has a light, soft sound, which is what you expect when you hear a ukulele. The larger the instrument, the deeper the sound is. Some tenor ukuleles have six or even eight strings.

The soprano ukulele is the most common, but you can use soprano, concert, and four-string tenor ukuleles with this book. Because the baritone ukulele is tuned to the same notes as the top four strings of the guitar, you can use *Learn to Play Baritone Uke* (Alfred item 380) to start learning.

THE PARTS OF YOUR UKULELE

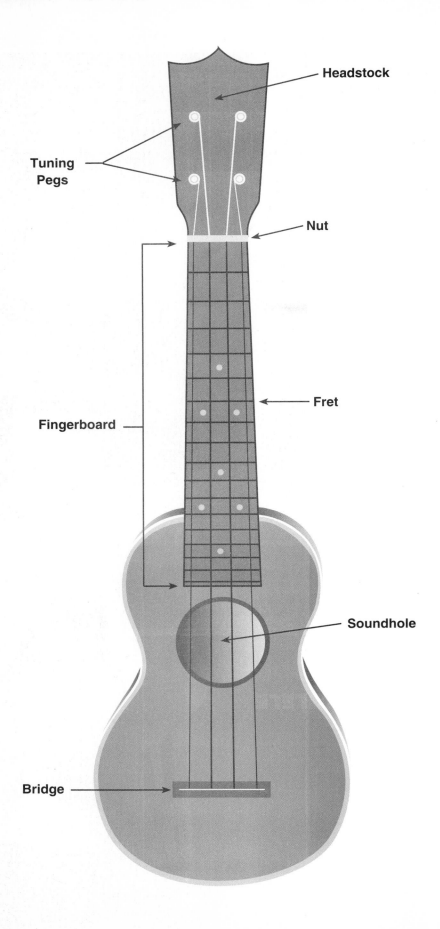

Headstock

Tuning Pegs

Nut

Fret

Fingerboard

Soundhole

Bridge

HOW TO HOLD YOUR UKULELE

Standing

Cradle the ukulele with your right arm by gently holding it close to your body. Your right hand should be free to strum it. Keep your left wrist away from the fingerboard. This allows your fingers to be in a better position to finger the chords.

Sitting

Rest the ukulele gently on your thigh.

THE RIGHT HAND: STRUMMING THE STRINGS

To *strum* means to play the strings with your right hand by brushing quickly across them. There are two common ways of strumming the strings. One is with a pick, and the other is with your fingers.

Strumming with a Pick

Hold the pick between your thumb and index finger. Hold it firmly, but don't squeeze it too hard.

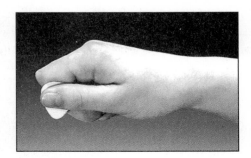

Strum from the 4th string (closest to the ceiling) to the 1st string (closest to the floor).

Important: Always strum by mostly moving your wrist, not just your arm. Use as little motion as possible. Start as close to the top strings as you can, and never let your hand move past the edge of the ukulele.

Start near the top string.

Move mostly your wrist, not just your arm.
Finish near the bottom string.

Strumming with Your Fingers

Decide if you feel more comfortable strumming with the side of your thumb or the nail of your index finger. The strumming motion is the same with the thumb or finger as it is when using the pick. Strum from the 4th string to the 1st string.

Strumming with the thumb.

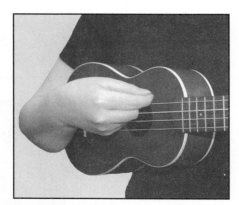

Strumming with the index finger.

USING YOUR LEFT HAND

Hand Position

Learning to use your left-hand fingers easily starts with a good hand position. Place your hand so your thumb rests comfortably in the middle of the back of the neck. Position your fingers on the front of the neck as if you are gently squeezing a ball between them and your thumb. Keep your elbow in and your fingers curved.

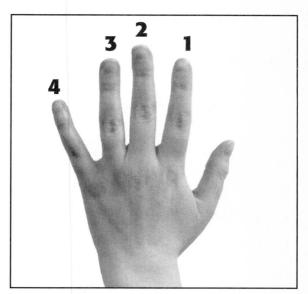

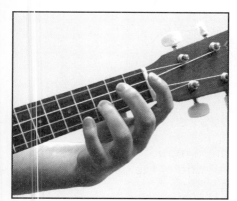

Keep elbow in and fingers curved.

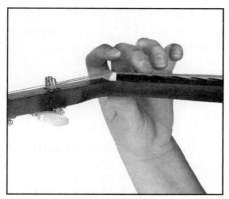

Like gently squeezing a ball between your fingers and thumb.

Finger numbers.

Placing a Finger on a String

When you press a string with a left-hand finger, make sure you press firmly with the tip of your finger and as close to the fret wire as you can without actually being right on it. Short fingernails are important! This will create a clean, bright tone.

RIGHT
Finger pressing the string down near the fret without actually being on it.

WRONG
Finger is too far from fret wire; tone is "buzzy" and indefinite.

WRONG
Finger is on top of fret wire; tone is muffled and unclear.

HOW TO TUNE YOUR UKULELE

Make sure your strings are wound properly around the tuning pegs. They should go from the inside to the outside, as in the picture.

Tuning a tuning peg clockwise makes the pitch lower. Turning a tuning peg counter-clockwise makes the pitch higher. Be sure not to tune the strings too high because they could break!

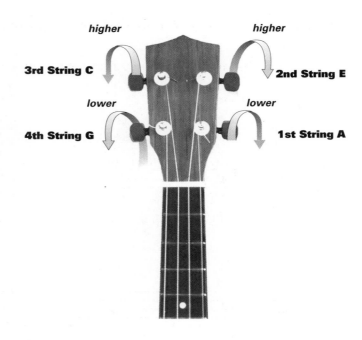

Important:

Always remember that the string closest to the floor is the 1st string. The one closest to the ceiling is the 4th string.

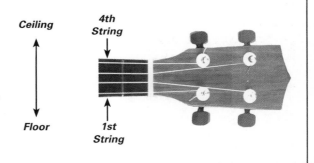

Tuning with the MP3 Audio or the DVD

Track 1

To tune using the MP3 audio (see page 2), play track 1. Listen to the directions and match each of your ukulele's strings to the corresponding pitches.

To use the DVD, go to the "Scene Selection" menu and click "How To Tune Your Ukulele." Follow the directions, and listen carefully to get your ukulele in tune.

Tuning the Ukulele to Itself

When your 1st string is in tune, you can tune the rest of the strings just using the ukulele alone.
If you have a piano, or keyboard, available, then tune the 1st string to A on the piano, and then follow the instructions below to get the ukulele in tune.

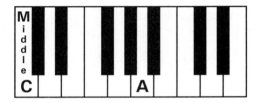

Press fret 5 of string 2 and tune it to the pitch of string 1 (A).

Press fret 4 of string 3 and tune it to the pitch of string 2 (E).

Press fret 2 of string 4 and tune it to the pitch of string 1 (A).

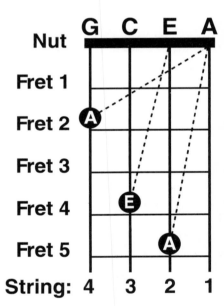

Pitch Pipes and Electronic Tuners

If you don't have a piano available, buying an electronic tuner or pitch pipe is recommended.
The salesperson at your local music store can show you how to use them.

GETTING ACQUAINTED WITH MUSIC

Musical sounds are indicated by symbols called *notes*. Their time value is determined by their color (white or black) and by stems or flags attached to the note.

The Staff

The notes are named after the first seven letters of the alphabet (A–G), repeated to embrace the entire range of musical sound. The name and pitch of the note is determined by its position on five horizontal lines, and the spaces between, called the *staff*.

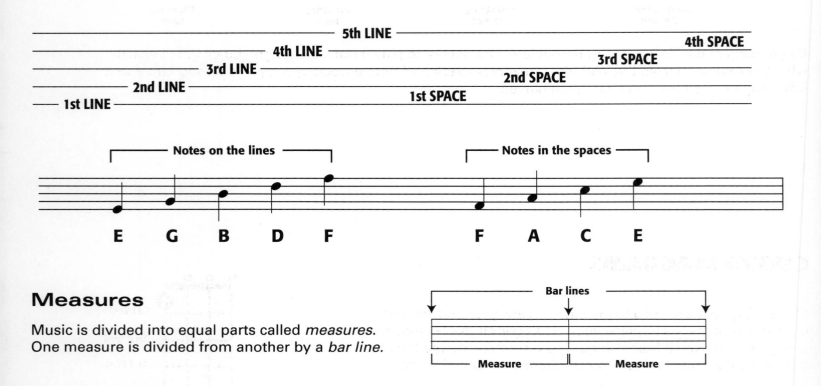

Measures

Music is divided into equal parts called *measures*. One measure is divided from another by a *bar line*.

Clefs

During the evolution of musical notation, the staff had from 2 to 20 lines, and symbols were invented to locate certain lines and the pitch of the note on that line. These symbols are called *clefs*.

Music for ukulele is written in the *G clef* or *treble clef*. Originally, the Gothic letter G was used on a four-line staff to establish the pitch of G.

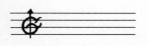   This grew into the modern notation:

READING TAB

All the music in this book is written two ways: in standard music notation and TAB.

Below each standard music staff you'll find a four-line TAB staff. Each line represents a string of the ukulele, with the 1st string at the top and the 4th string at the bottom.

— 1st string
— 2nd string
— 3rd string
— 4th string

Numbers placed on the TAB lines tell you which fret to play. An o means to play the string open (not fingered).

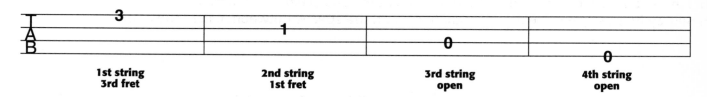

| 1st string | 2nd string | 3rd string | 4th string |
| 3rd fret | 1st fret | open | open |

By glancing at the TAB, you can immediately tell where to play a note. Although you can't tell exactly what the rhythm is from the TAB, the horizontal spacing of the numbers gives you a strong hint about how long or short the notes are to be played.

CHORD DIAGRAMS

Chord diagrams are used to indicate fingering for chords. The example here means to place your 1st finger on the 1st fret, 1st string, then strum all four strings. The o symbols on the 2nd, 3rd, and 4th strings indicate to play them open (not fingered).

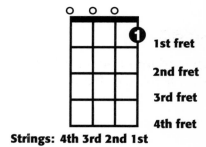

1st fret
2nd fret
3rd fret
4th fret

Strings: 4th 3rd 2nd 1st

THE FIRST STRING A Track 2

OPEN STRING
(not fingered)

 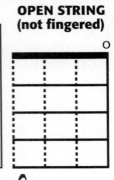 **2nd FRET**  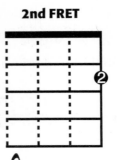  **2nd FRET**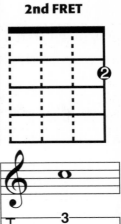

A   **B**   **C**

Play slowly and evenly. Use only down-strokes, indicated by ⊓.
Remember, the symbol ○ over a note means *open string*. Do not finger.

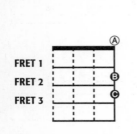

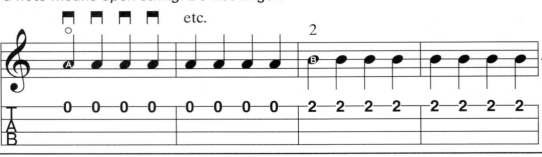

Playing with A, B, and C Track 3

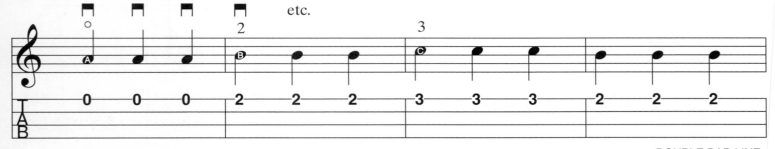

DOUBLE BAR LINE

USED TO SIGNAL THE
END OF THE PIECE

EXTRA CREDIT Track 4

Make sure to place your left-hand fingers as close to the fret wires as possible without touching them. When you play the B on the 2nd fret and follow it with the C on the 3rd fret, keep your 2nd finger down. You will only hear the C, but when you go back to the B, it will sound smooth.

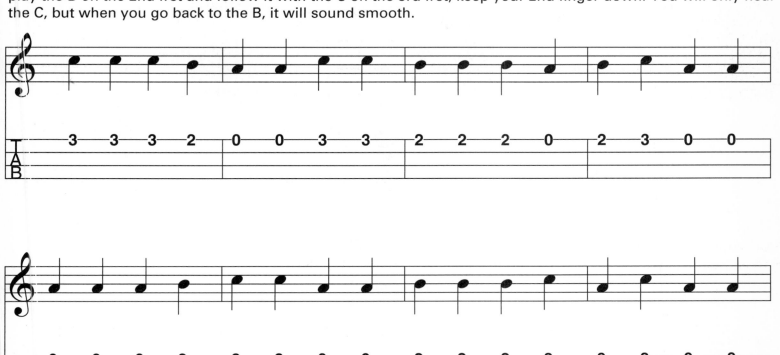

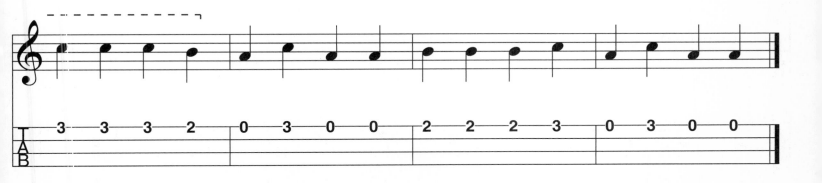

SOUND-OFF: HOW TO COUNT TIME

4 Kinds of Notes

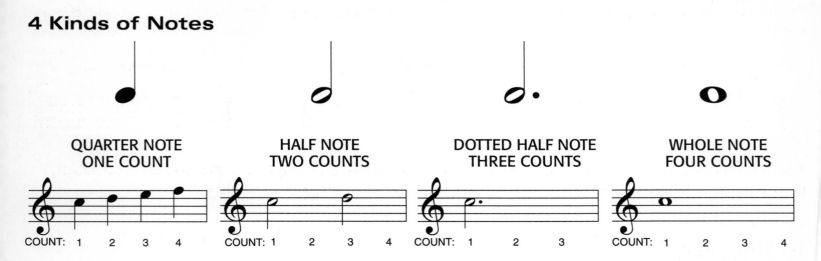

Time Signatures

Each piece of music has numbers at the beginning called a *time signature*. These numbers tell us how to count time. The TOP NUMBER tells us how many counts are in each measure. The BOTTOM NUMBER tells us what kind of note gets one count.

FOUR COUNTS TO A MEASURE

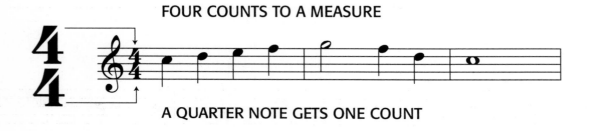

A QUARTER NOTE GETS ONE COUNT

THREE COUNTS TO A MEASURE

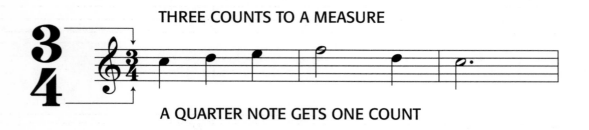

A QUARTER NOTE GETS ONE COUNT

TWO COUNTS TO A MEASURE

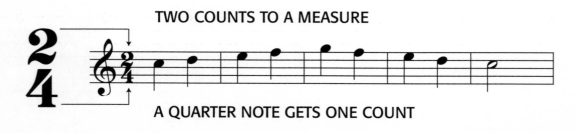

A QUARTER NOTE GETS ONE COUNT

Important: Go back and fill in the missing time signatures of the songs already learned.

REPEAT SIGNS

This music uses *repeat signs*. The double dots inside the double bars tell you that everything in between those double bars is to be repeated.

 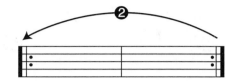 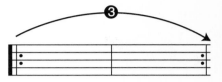

The best way to learn all the songs and exercises is to listen to the recording first so that you can hear exactly what is going to happen. Follow along in the music as you listen. Then, enjoy playing along.

1st String Blues

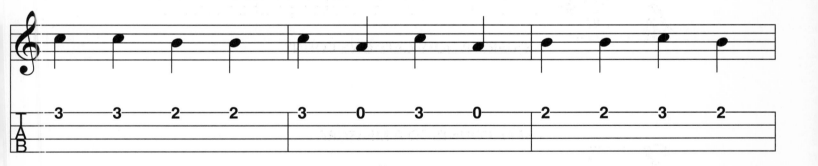

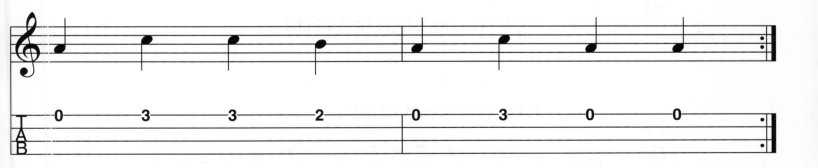

THE SECOND STRING E

Track 6

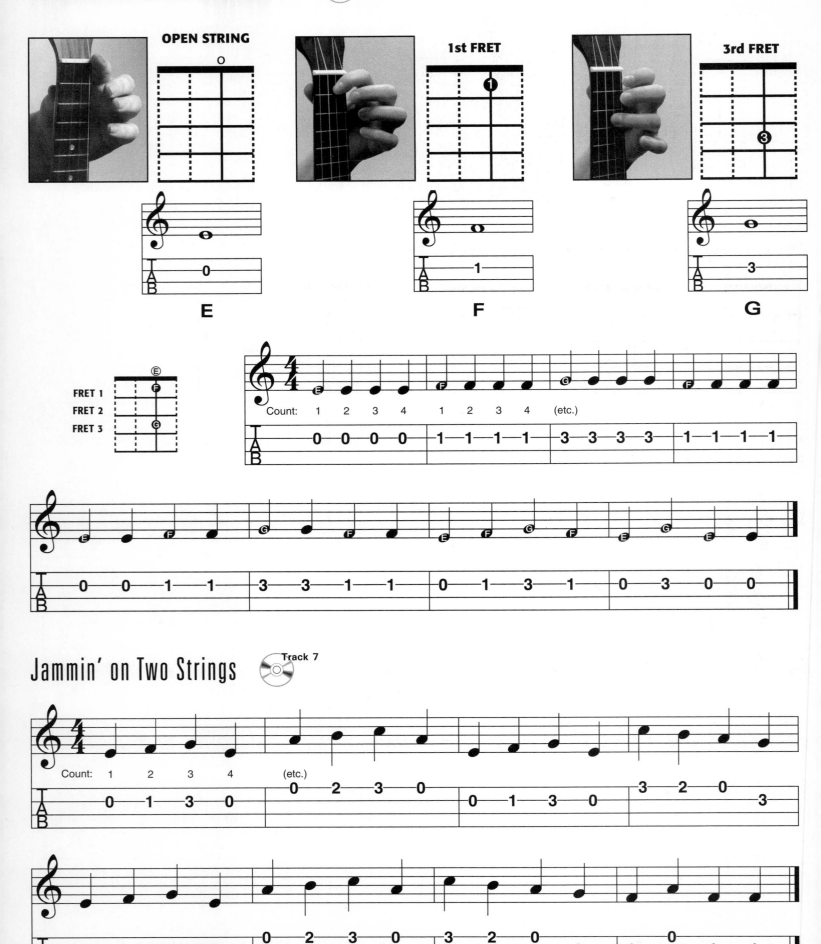

OPEN STRING   1st FRET   3rd FRET

E   F   G

Jammin' on Two Strings

Track 7

Hot Cross Buns

Track 8

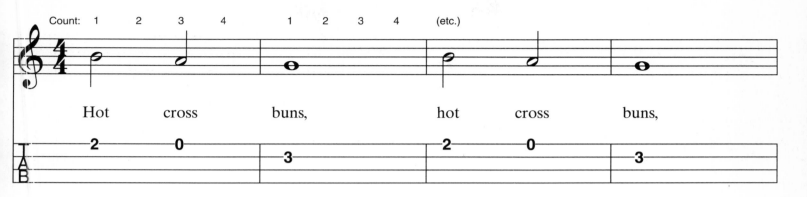

Hot cross buns, hot cross buns,

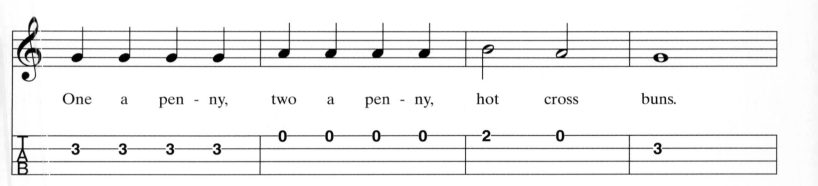

One a pen - ny, two a pen - ny, hot cross buns.

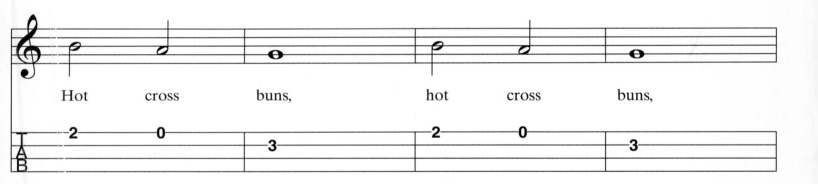

Hot cross buns, hot cross buns,

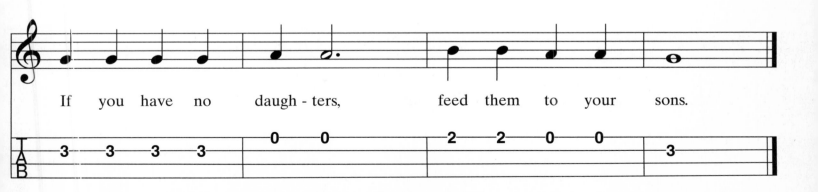

If you have no daugh - ters, feed them to your sons.

Blues in C

Track 9

If you have a friend or teacher and he or she wants to play along with you, the chord symbols above each staff may be used for a teacher-student duet. These chords are not to be played by the student.

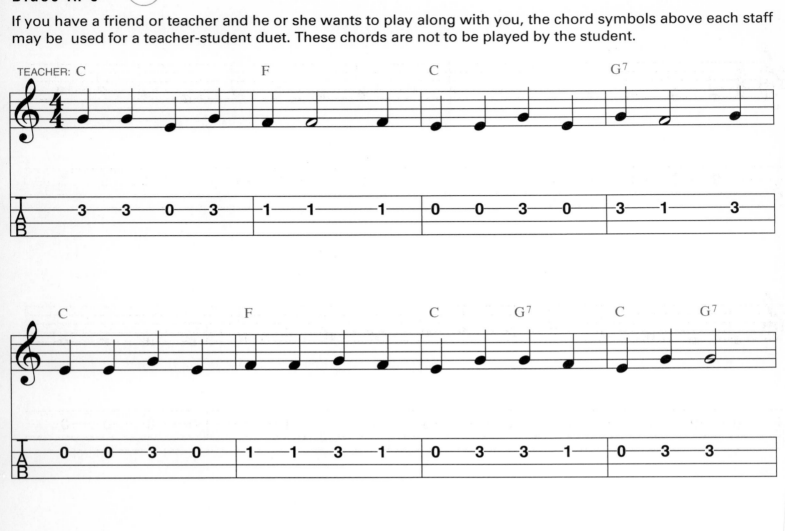

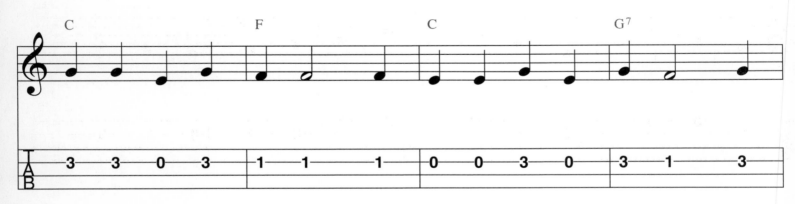

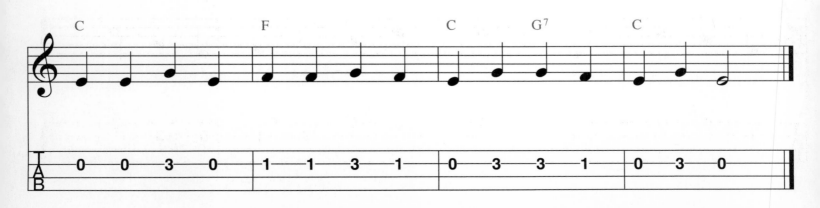

Rockin' Uke

Track 10

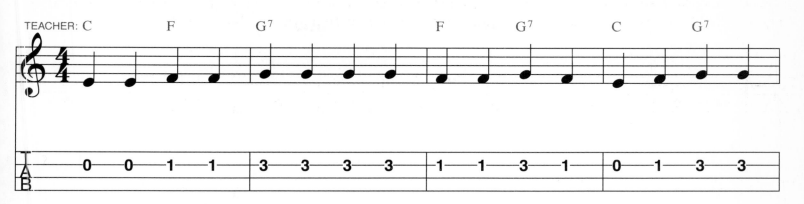

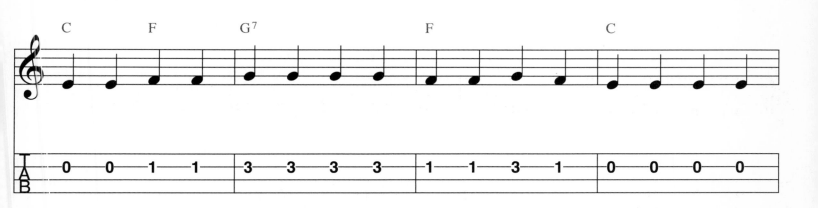

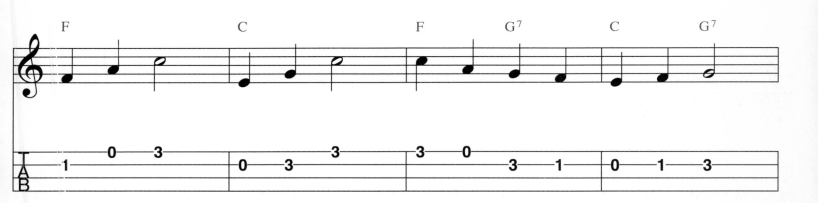

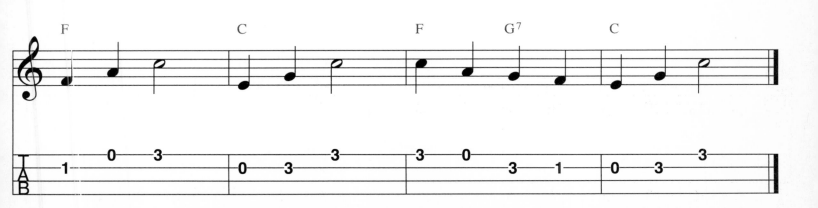

THE THIRD STRING C Track 11

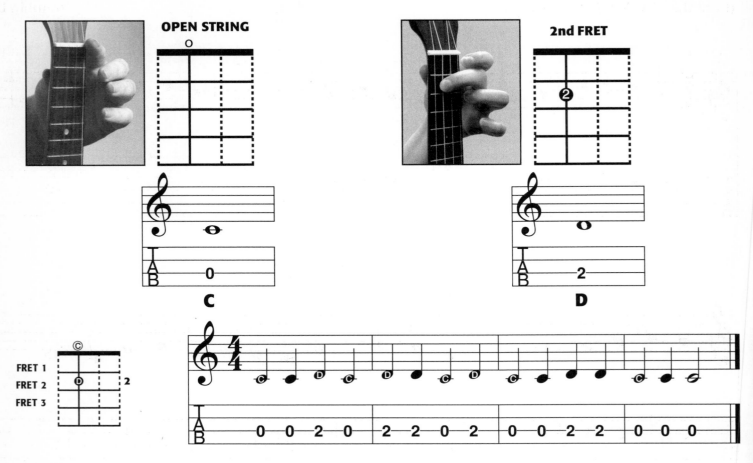

OPEN STRING

2nd FRET

C

D

Jammin' on Three Strings Track 12

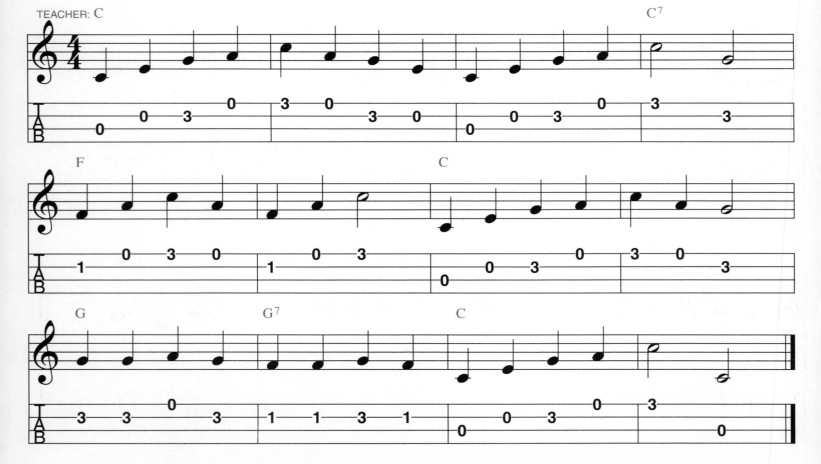

Largo

Track 13

(from the *New World Symphony*)

Antonin Dvořák

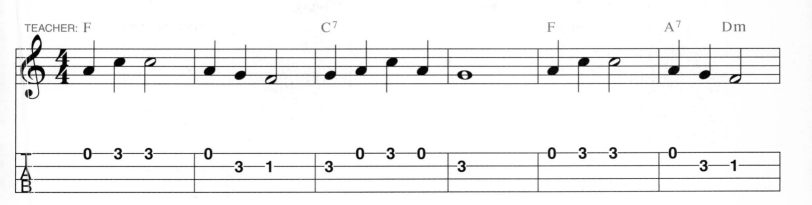

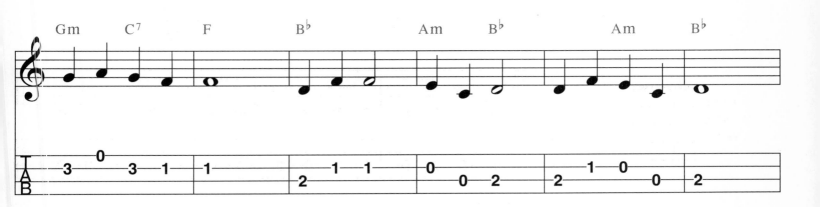

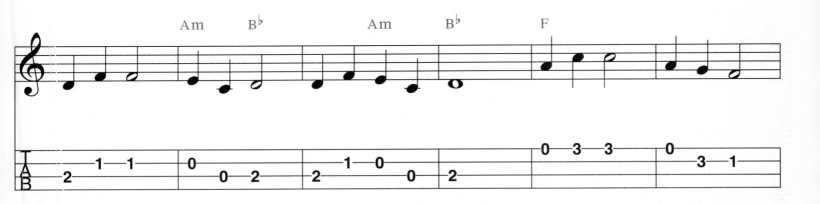

Jingle Bells

Track 14

TEACHER: C

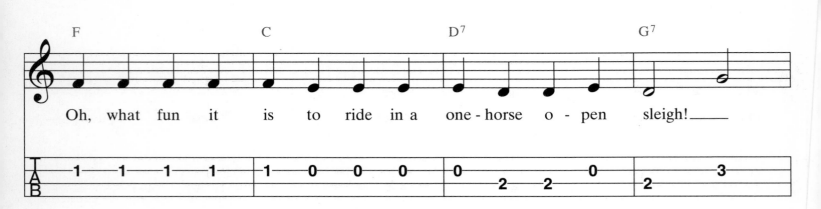

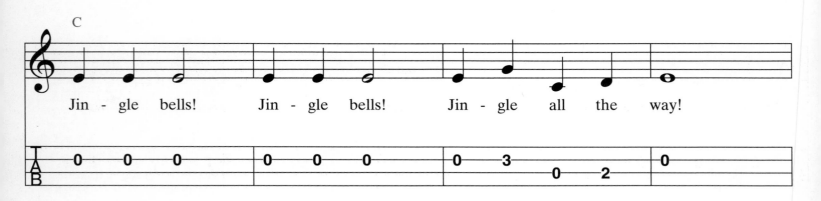

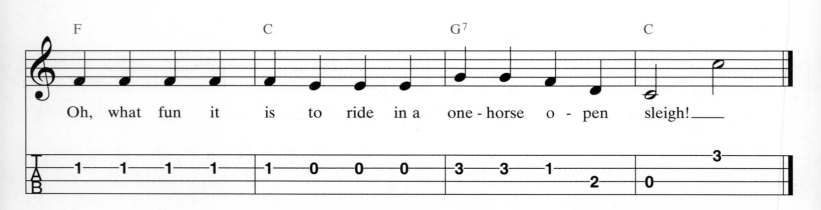

Beautiful Brown Eyes

Track 15

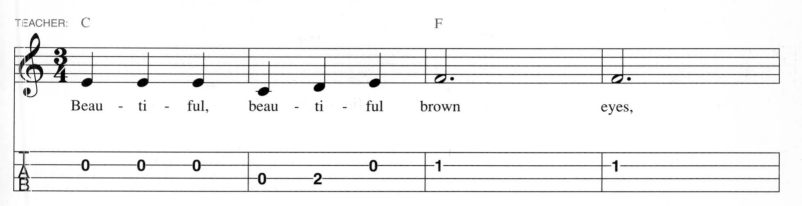

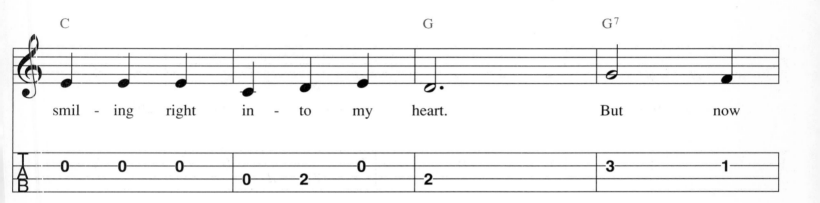

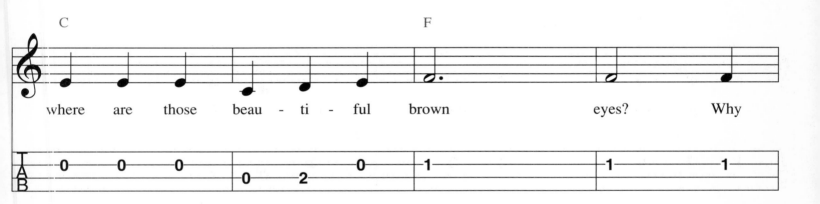

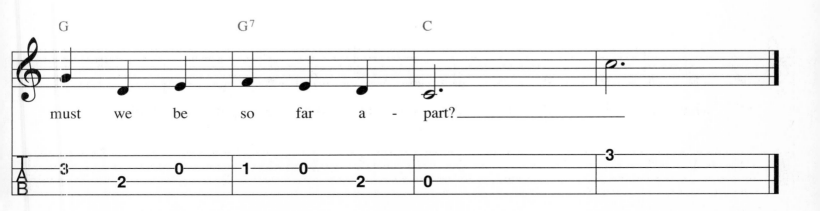

INTRODUCING B-FLAT Track 16

A *flat* ♭ lowers a note a half step. B♭ is played one fret lower than the note B. When a flat note appears in a measure, it is still flat until the end of that measure.

1st FRET

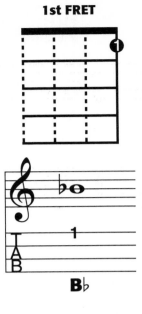

B♭

Aura Lee Track 17

This old American folk song was later recorded by Elvis Presley and called "Love Me Tender."

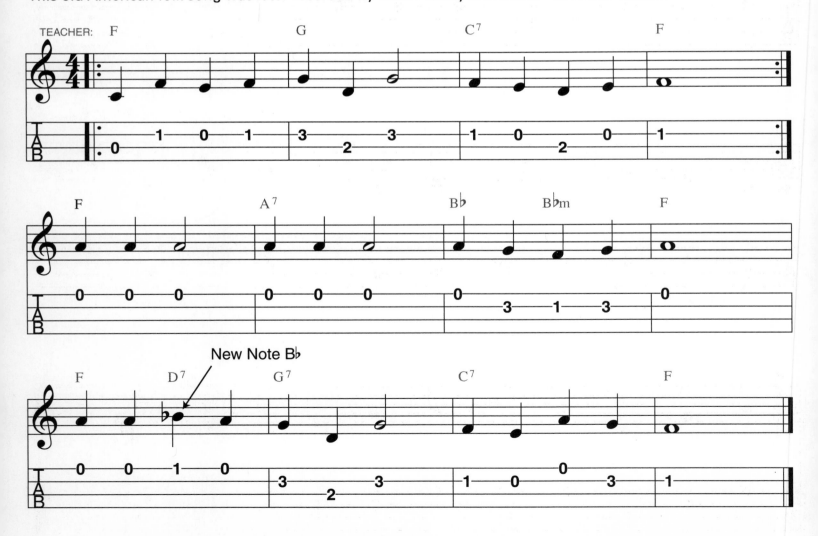

Three-String Boogie

Track 18

This song uses all the notes you have learned. Don't forget to listen to the MP3 audio or DVD first!

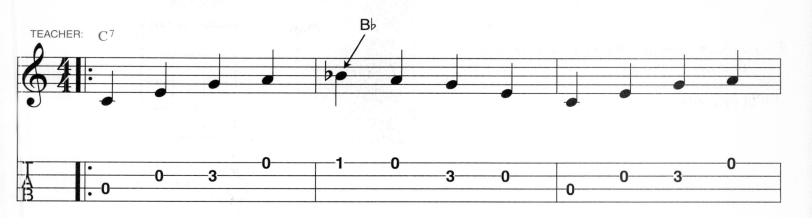

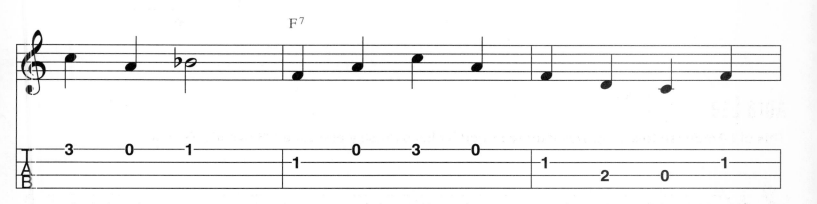

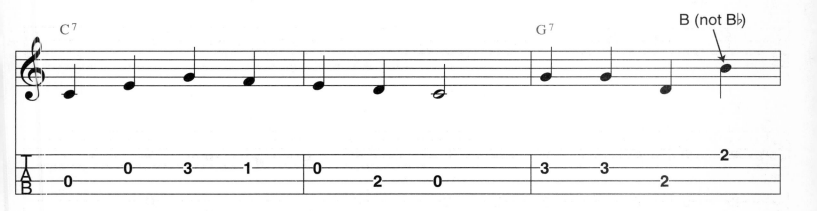

TEMPO SIGNS

A *tempo sign* tells you how fast to play the music. Below are the three most common tempo signs, which are Italian words. In some music, you will see tempo signs written in English.

Andante ("ahn-DAHN-teh") means to play slow.

Moderato ("moh-deh-RAH-toh") means to play moderately.

Allegro ("ah-LAY-groh") means to play fast.

Quarter Rest

This sign indicates silence for one count. For a clearer effect, you may stop the sound of the strings by touching the strings lightly with the heel of the right hand.

Three-Tempo Rockin' Uke

Track 19

Play three times: first time **Andante**, second time **Moderato**, third time **Allegro**.

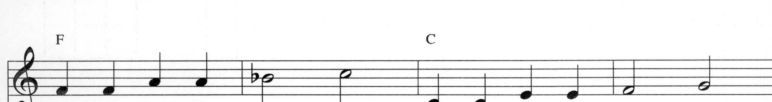

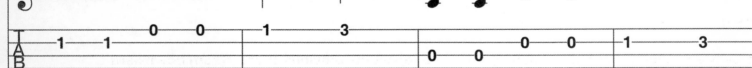

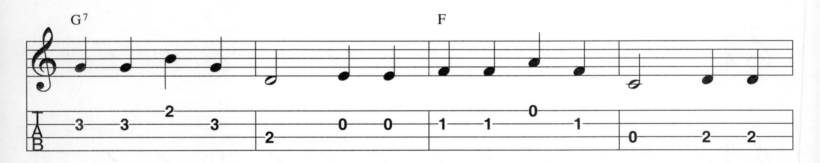

Count: 1   2   3   (rest)

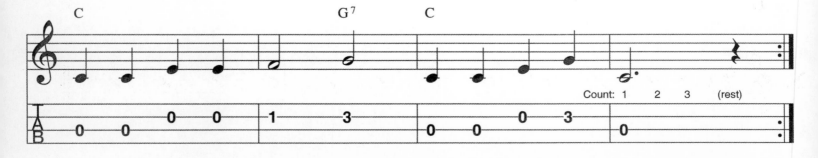

THE C7 CHORD

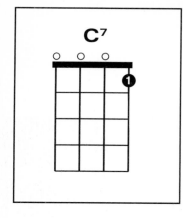

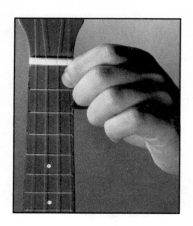

o = open string

- - - - - - - - - = string is not played

Place your 1st finger in position, then play one string at a time.

Play all four
strings together:

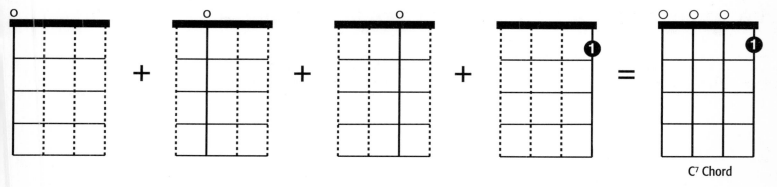

C⁷ Chord

Track 21

Play slowly and evenly. Each slash mark ╱ means to repeat the previous chord. Strum downward
for each chord name and slash mark. Use your finger or a pick. The chord name is repeated in each measure.

1. 𝄞 2/4 C⁷ ╱ | C⁷ ╱ | C⁷ ╱ | C⁷ ╱ | C⁷ ╱ | C⁷ ╱ ‖

2. 𝄞 3/4 C⁷ ╱ ╱ | C⁷ ╱ ╱ | C⁷ ╱ ╱ | C⁷ ╱ ╱ ‖

3. 𝄞 4/4 C⁷ ╱ ╱ ╱ | C⁷ ╱ ╱ ╱ | C⁷ ╱ ╱ ╱ ‖

THE F CHORD Track 22

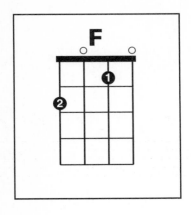

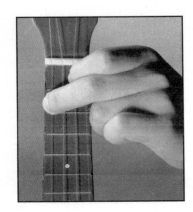

Place your 1st and 2nd fingers in position, then play one string at a time.

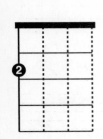 + 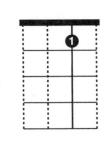 + 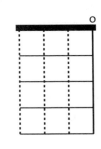 + 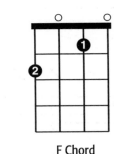 = F Chord

 Track 23

1. $\frac{2}{4}$ | F ╱ | F ╱ | F ╱ | F ╱ | F ╱ | F ╱ ‖

2. $\frac{3}{4}$ | F ╱ ╱ | F ╱ ╱ | F ╱ ╱ | F ╱ ╱ ‖

3. $\frac{4}{4}$ | F ╱ ╱ ╱ | F ╱ ╱ ╱ | F ╱ ╱ ╱ ‖

 Track 24

Once you can play both the F and C7 chords clearly, try combining them as in the following exercises.

1. $\frac{4}{4}$ | F ╱╱╱ | F ╱╱╱ | C⁷ ╱╱╱ | C⁷ ╱╱╱ | F ╱╱╱ | C⁷ ╱╱╱ | F ╱╱╱ | F ‖
   HOLD

2. $\frac{3}{4}$ | F ╱╱ | F ╱╱ | C⁷ ╱╱ | C⁷ ╱╱ | F ╱╱ | C⁷ ╱╱ | F ╱╱ | F 𝄽 𝄽 ‖
   COUNT: 1 REST REST

3. $\frac{2}{4}$ | F ╱ | F ╱ | C⁷ ╱ | C⁷ ╱ | F ╱ | C⁷ ╱ | F ╱ | F ╱ ‖

Good Night Ladies

Track 25
Vocals & Chords

Track 26
Chords only

For this song and most of the rest of the songs in this book, you can play either the melody or chords. Your teacher can play the part you aren't playing, or you can play along with the MP3 audio or DVD.

Moderato

KEY SIGNATURES

The *key signature* at the beginning of a piece tells you when a note is played as a flat note throughout the piece. In "Down in the Valley," each B is played as B-flat.

Ties

This curved line is called a *tie*. It connects two or more notes and ties them together. Play or sing the note once and hold it for the value of both (or more) tied notes.

In TAB, a tied note is shown as a number in parentheses. Do not pick the note again.

Down in the Valley

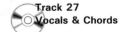 Track 27
Vocals & Chords

 Track 28
Chords only

Key Signature: remember to play each B one half step lower.

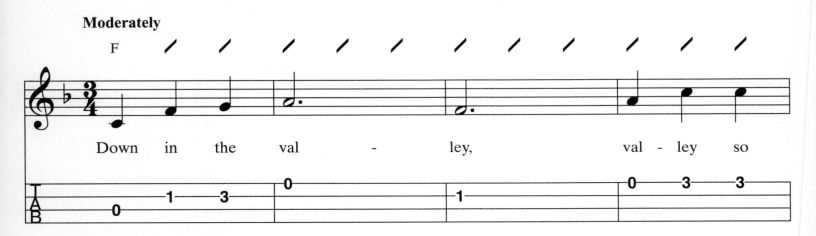

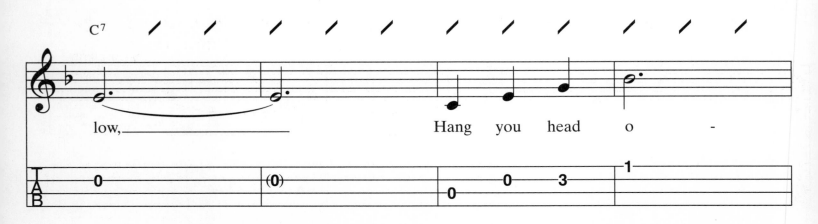

Ode to Joy

Theme from Beethoven's *Ninth Symphony*

Track 29
Vocals & Chords

Track 30
Chords only

THE C CHORD

 Track 31

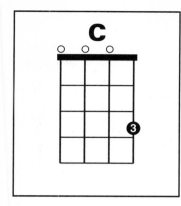

Place your 3rd finger in position, then play one string at a time.

Play all four strings together:

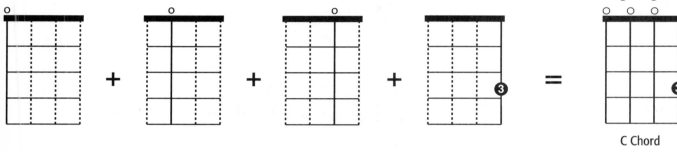

C Chord

Play slowly and evenly. **Track 32**

Now try these exercise. They combine all the chords you know. **Track 33**

INCOMPLETE MEASURES

Not all pieces of music begin on the first beat. Sometimes, music begins with an incomplete measure called a *pickup*. If the pickup is one beat, often the last measure will only have three beats in $\frac{4}{4}$, or two beats in $\frac{3}{4}$.

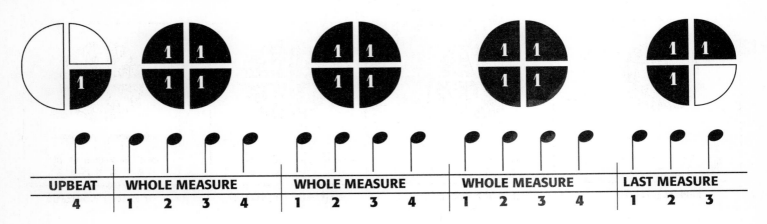

UPBEAT	WHOLE MEASURE				WHOLE MEASURE				WHOLE MEASURE				LAST MEASURE		
4	1	2	3	4	1	2	3	4	1	2	3	4	1	2	3

A-Tisket, A-Tasket

Track 34
Vocals & Chords

Track 35
Chords only

Allegro

EIGHTH NOTES

Eighth notes are black notes that have a flag added to the stem: ♪ or ♩.

Two or more eighth notes are written with a *beam*: ♫ or ♫. Each eighth note receives one half beat.

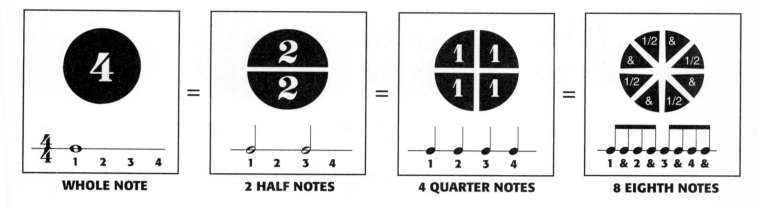

WHOLE NOTE = **2 HALF NOTES** = **4 QUARTER NOTES** = **8 EIGHTH NOTES**

Use alternating down-strokes ⊓ and up-strokes ∨ on eighth notes.

Track 36

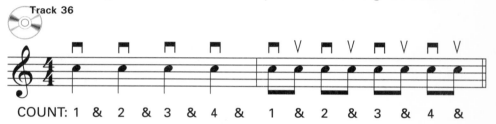

COUNT: 1 & 2 & 3 & 4 & 1 & 2 & 3 & 4 &

Jammin' with Eighth Notes

Track 37
Vocals & Chords

Track 38
Chords only

Allegro moderato*

*Allegro moderato means moderately fast.

DOTTED QUARTER NOTES

A DOT INCREASES
THE LENGTH OF A
NOTE BY ONE HALF

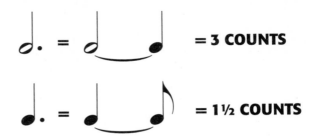

Preparatory Drill

The only difference in the
following two measures and
those directly above them is
the way they are written. They
should sound the SAME.

Cockles and Mussels

Track 39
Vocals & Chords

Track 40
Chords only

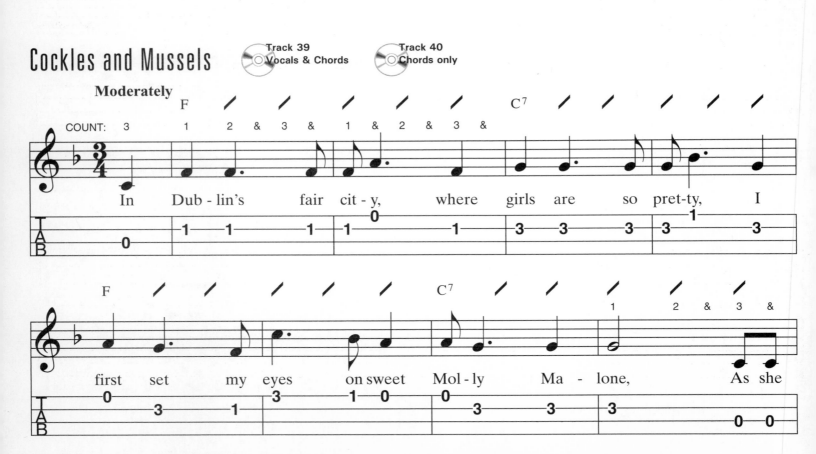

In Dub - lin's fair cit - y, where girls are so pret-ty, I first set my eyes on sweet Mol - ly Ma - lone, As she

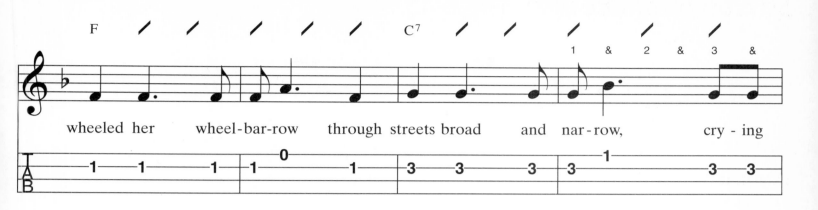

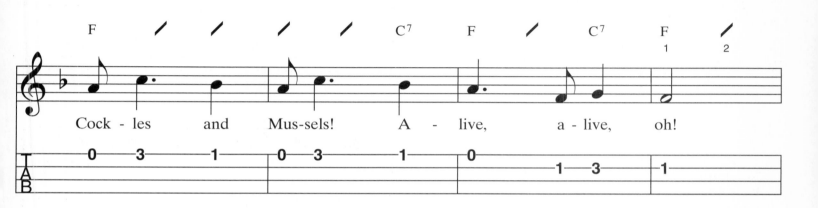

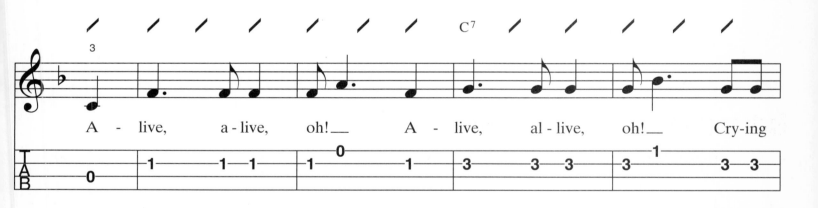

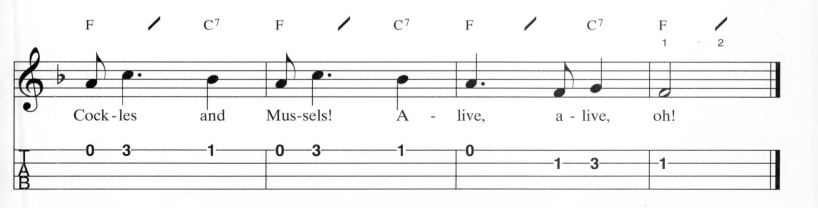

Clementine

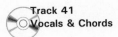 Track 41
Vocals & Chords

 Track 42
Chords only

Moderately fast

Count: 3 & 1 2 3 &

In a cav - ern, in a can - yon, ex - ca - vat - ing for a

mine, lived a min - er, for - ty - nin - er, and his

daugh - ter, Clem - en - tine. Oh my dar - lin', oh my

dar - lin', oh my dar - lin', Clem - en - tine, you are

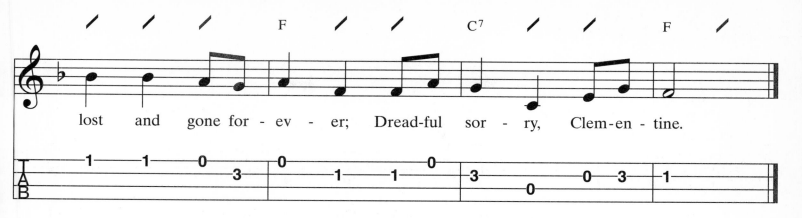

lost and gone for - ev - er; Dread-ful sor - ry, Clem-en - tine.

ADDITIONAL VERSES

Verse 2:

Light she was and like fairy,
And her shows were number nine,
Herring boxes without topses,
Sandals were for Clementine

Chorus:

Oh my darling, oh my darling,
Oh my darling, Clementine!
Thou art lost and gone forever
Dreadful sorry, Clementine.

Verse 3:

Drove she ducklings to the water
Every morning just at nine,
Hit her foot against a splinter,
Fell into the foaming brine.

Chorus:

Oh my darling, oh my darling
Oh my darling, Clementine!
Thou art lost and gone forever
Dreadful sorry, Clementine.

Verse 4:

Ruby lips above the water,
Blowing bubbles soft and fine,
But alas, I was no swimmer,
So I lost my Clementine.

Chorus:

Oh my darling, oh my darling
Oh my darling, Clementine
Thou art lost and gone forever,
Dreadful sorry, Clementine.

THE G7 CHORD

Track 43

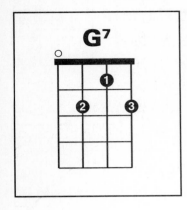

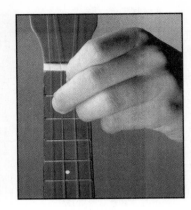

Place your 1st, 2nd, and 3rd fingers in position, then play one string at a time.

Play all four strings together:

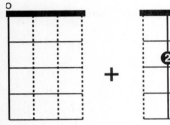 + 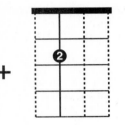 + 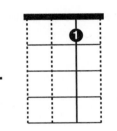 + 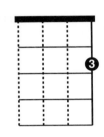 =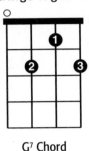

G⁷ Chord

Track 44

Play slowly and evenly.

1. 𝄞 4/4 | G⁷ ╱ ╱ ╱ | C ╱ ╱ ╱ | G⁷ ╱ ╱ ╱ | C ╱ ╱ ╱ |

2. 𝄞 3/4 | C ╱ ╱ | G⁷ ╱ ╱ | C ╱ ╱ | G⁷ ╱ ╱ | C ╱ ╱ | C 𝄽 𝄽 ‖

3. 𝄞 2/4 | G⁷ ╱ | C ╱ | G⁷ ╱ | C ╱ | F ╱ | C ╱ | G⁷ ╱ | C ╱ ‖

4. 𝄞 4/4 | C ╱ ╱ ╱ | F ╱ ╱ ╱ | C ╱ ╱ ╱ | G⁷ ╱ ╱ ╱ | C ╱ ╱ ╱ | C ╱ ╱ 𝄽 ‖

5. 𝄞 3/4 | C ╱ ╱ | C⁷ ╱ ╱ | F ╱ ╱ | C ╱ ╱ | F ╱ ╱ | F ╱ ╱ | C ╱ ╱ | C ╱ ╱ |

| G⁷ ╱ ╱ | G⁷ ╱ ╱ | C ╱ ╱ | F ╱ ╱ | C ╱ ╱ | C 𝄽 𝄽 ‖

Aloha 'Oe
Track 45

(Farewell to Thee)

To get used to playing the G7 chord, play this version of "Aloha 'Oe" (pronounced "oy") with just chords. Sing along with the melody.

This arrangement uses quarter note slashes that indicate to play one strum on each quarter note.

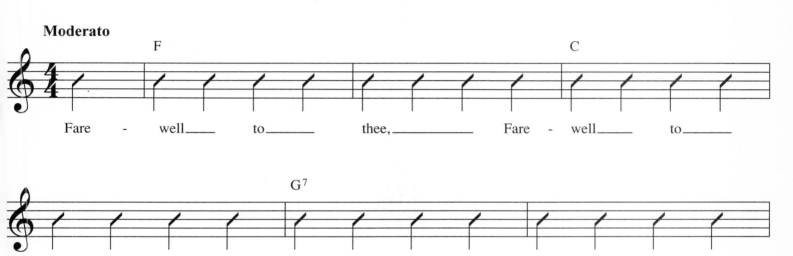

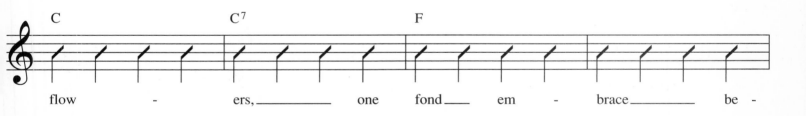

When the Saints Go Marching In

Track 46
Vocals & Chords

Track 47
Chords only

Love Somebody

Track 48
Vocals & Chords

Track 49
Chords only

Moderately

The Streets of Laredo

Track 50 — Vocals & Chords Track 51 — Chords only

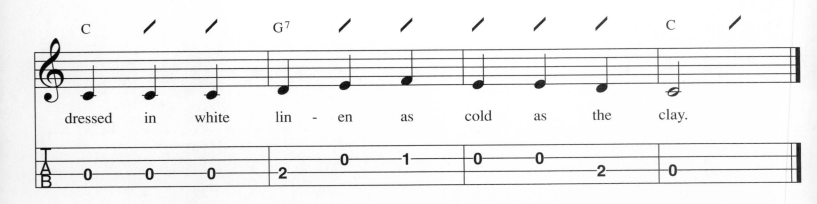

THE DOWN-AND-UP STROKE

Track 52

You can make your accompaniment of waltz songs in $\frac{3}{4}$ like "The Streets of Laredo" more interesting by replacing the second beat of the measure with a down-stroke followed by an up-stroke. Together, the down-and-up strokes are played in the same time as a regular strum.

Try the following exercise to work on just the rhythm.

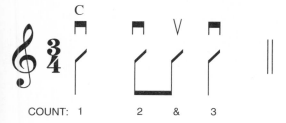

Now practice changing from C to G7.

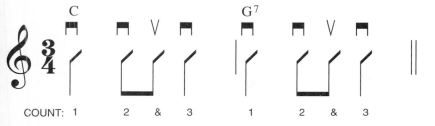

Now practice changing back and forth from C to G7 and back. When you can do it smoothly, go back to page 44 and use it to accompany "The Streets of Laredo."

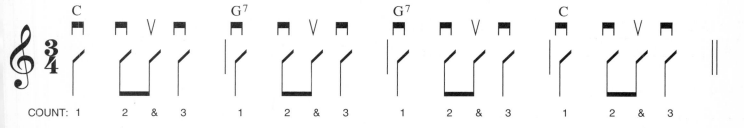

46

THE G CHORD

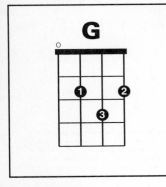
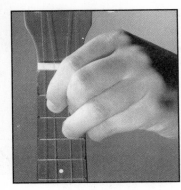

Place your 1st, 2nd, and 3rd fingers in position, then play one string at a time.

Play all four strings together:

 + 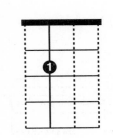 + 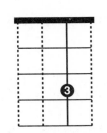 + 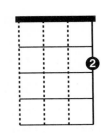 =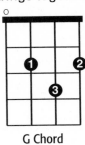

G Chord

THE D7 CHORD

Place your 1st and 2nd fingers in position, then play one string at a time.

Play all four strings together:

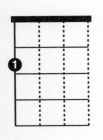 + 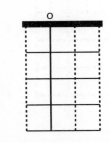 +  + 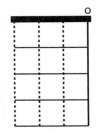 =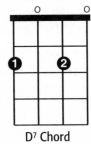

D⁷ Chord

Calypso Strum

 Track 55

The calypso strum is used to accompany Caribbean songs like "Mary Ann," "Jamaica Farewell," and "The Sloop John B." The rhythm is a little tricky, so make sure you can play the exercises on this page before trying the song on the following page.

Play a steady four-to-the-bar pattern on a C chord. Use only down-strokes.

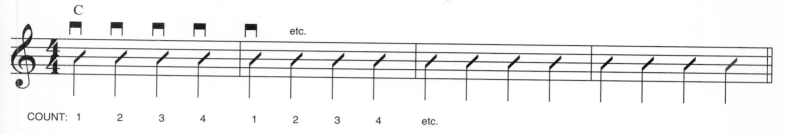

COUNT: 1   2   3   4   1   2   3   4   etc.

Now add an eighth note up-stroke after each down-stroke. Notice how the count has changed.

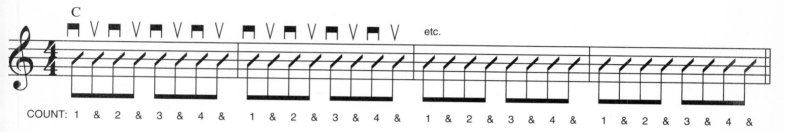

COUNT: 1 & 2 & 3 & 4 &   1 & 2 & 3 & 4 &   1 & 2 & 3 & 4 &   1 & 2 & 3 & 4 &

Now leave out the down-stroke on beat 3 and replace it with an eighth rest (𝄾). Notice that you now have two up-strokes in a row on the "and" of 2 and the "and" of 3.

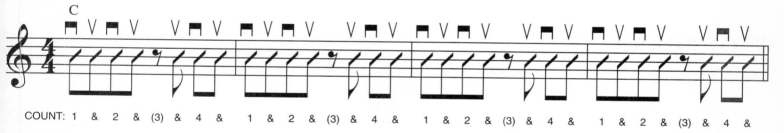

COUNT: 1 & 2 & (3) & 4 &   1 & 2 & (3) & 4 &   1 & 2 & (3) & 4 &   1 & 2 & (3) & 4 &

This whole pattern represents one measure of the calypso strum. As soon as you can do it without missing a beat, try "The Sloop John B."

INTRODUCING F-SHARP

 Track 56

A *sharp* ♯ raises a note a half step. F♯ is played one fret higher than the note F. When a sharp note appears in a measure, it is still sharp until the end of that measure.

Notice "The Sloop John B." on page 48 uses a key signature with one sharp. Key signatures can use either sharps or flats.

2nd FRET

F♯

The Sloop John B.

Track 57
Vocals & Chords

Track 58
Chords only

Start this song with the calypso strum to get into the rhythm of it.
Then start singing.